Early Praise for *JavaScript Brain Teasers*

The challenging, varied puzzles keep you reading, and the succinct explanations keep you learning. Loved every page of this surprisingly eclectic book on JavaScript.

➤ **Lukas Mathis**
Author of *Designed for Use*

A fun read about JavaScript's features and functions that may not be familiar to every user of the language. Both enjoyable and educational.

➤ **Marcus S. Zarra**
iOS/OS X Developer

I've been writing JavaScript for over decade now, and I learned things from this book. I like how the puzzles are not "gotcha" questions about obscure edge cases that topics like this can fall into—each one has a specific learning objective in mind.

➤ **Randall Koutnik**
Author of *Build Reactive Websites with RxJS*

JavaScript Brain Teasers

Exercise Your Mind

Faraz K. Kelhini

The Pragmatic Bookshelf

Dallas, Texas

When we are aware that a term used in this book is claimed as a trademark, the designation is printed with an initial capital letter or in all capitals.

The Pragmatic Starter Kit, The Pragmatic Programmer, Pragmatic Programming, Pragmatic Bookshelf, PragProg and the linking *g* device are trademarks of The Pragmatic Programmers, LLC.

Every precaution was taken in the preparation of this book. However, the publisher assumes no responsibility for errors or omissions, or for damages that may result from the use of information (including program listings) contained herein.

For our complete catalog of hands-on, practical, and Pragmatic content for software developers, please visit *https://pragprog.com*.

The team that produced this book includes:

Publisher:	Dave Thomas
COO:	Janet Furlow
Executive Editor:	Susannah Davidson
Series Editor:	Miki Tebeka
Development Editor:	Margaret Eldridge
Copy Editor:	Karen Galle
Layout:	Gilson Graphics

For sales, volume licensing, and support, please contact *support@pragprog.com*.

For international rights, please contact *rights@pragprog.com*.

ISBN-13: 979-8-88865-052-3
Book version: P1.0—March 2024

Contents

Part II — Crafting Puzzles

Acknowledgments

Thank you for embarking on this coding adventure with me. Writing a book is never a solitary endeavor; it's the culmination of the support, guidance, and encouragement of many individuals.

I extend my appreciation to the team at The Pragmatic Programmers, whose expertise transformed this vision into a reality. Special thanks to Margaret Eldridge for your meticulous editing and keen eye for detail, ensuring the quality and clarity of the content.

Many thanks are owed to the experts Michael Fazio, Andy Lester, and Daniel Posey for their invaluable reviews of the book before it went to print. Their expertise as developers provided crucial insights into code quality.

I'd also like to express my appreciation to Randall Koutnik, Lukas Mathis, and Marcus S. Zarra. They not only took the time to review my book and highlight any errors I made but also offered kind words of encouragement and praise.

Preface

JavaScript has historically been known for its quirks and idiosyncrasies. These unusual characteristics often arise from its evolution as a language and the need to maintain backward compatibility, among other factors. For instance, a notable quirk in JavaScript is type coercion: JavaScript tries to be forgiving with data types, which can lead to unexpected behavior when different types are mixed.

It's important for developers to be aware of these aspects of JavaScript in order to write more robust and predictable code. Fortunately, the ECMAScript standard, which defines JavaScript, is evolving to address many of these issues and introducing more predictable behavior and additional features to the language.

In this book, we invite you on a journey through a carefully curated collection of intriguing JavaScript challenges, designed to unveil the intricate nuances and peculiarities that define the language's essence. Whether you are an advanced beginner seeking growth or a seasoned developer looking to sharpen your skills, there's something for you within these pages.

At the start of each chapter, I'll toss a cool little JavaScript program your way and challenge you to guess what it's going to output. Don't worry, I won't leave you hanging. After your best guess, feel free to run the code and see the magic happen! Then, go ahead and check out the explanation to level up your JavaScript skills.

About the Author

Faraz K. Kelhini is the author of Modern Asynchronous JavaScript and Text Processing with JavaScript. With a profound understanding of the JavaScript language and its intricate APIs, Faraz's journey has been fueled by a passion for championing innovative ideas that improve the coding experience, all while crafting solutions that seamlessly harmonize creativity and functionality.

About You

Before we embark on this exciting journey, it's essential to note some familiarity with JavaScript will greatly enhance your understanding of the concepts discussed here. If you're new to JavaScript and have never had the opportunity to explore its wonders, I recommend taking some time to learn the basics first—you'll find it to be an enjoyable experience!

About the Code

The provided code examples are designed to be concise and intended to demonstrate the core essence of each brain teaser. Feel free to execute these examples in your browser's console, but ensure that your browser is updated to the latest version.

To access the sample code featured in the book, please visit the Pragmatic Bookshelf website.[1] There, you can provide feedback, report any errors, get up-to-date information, and join in the discussions on the book's dedicated forum page.

If you're reading the book in PDF format, you can view or retrieve a particular example by selecting the small gray box located above the code segment.

---

1. https://www.pragprog.com/titles/fkjsbrain

Part I

JavaScript Brain Teasers

Your Code Deserves a Lift

your_code_deserves_a_lift/your_code_deserves_a_lift.js

```javascript
let temp = 25;

function displayTemperature() {
  console.log(`Current temperature: ${temp} °C`);
}

function forecastTemperature() {
  console.log(`Expected temperature: ${temp} °C`);
  var temp = 28;
}

displayTemperature();
forecastTemperature();
```

Guess the Output

 Try to guess what the output is before moving to the next page.

You might have expected the output to be:

```
Current temperature: 25 °C
Expected temperature: 25 °C
```

But this code will actually output:

```
Current temperature: 25 °C
Expected temperature: undefined °C
```

Discussion

In JavaScript, all declarations are subject to *hoisting*. This includes var, let, const, function, function*, and class declarations. Hoisting involves the automatic relocation of these declarations to the scope's beginning. But, their initialization is deferred until the execution flow hits the line where hoisting occurred. This process occurs before the code is executed, and it helps JavaScript handle references to variables and functions.

Consider the following code:

```
// Create a variable
var a = 10;
```

This code is processed by JavaScript in the following manner:

```
var a;
// Create a variable
a = 10;
```

When you declare a variable using the var keyword, the declaration is moved (or "hoisted") to the top of the containing function or global scope. However, the assignment (initialization) of the variable remains in its original place. This means that you can reference a var before it's declared in your code without causing an error. However, the value will be undefined until you actually assign a value to it.

This behavior can lead to unexpected outcomes when working with functions. Any variable that is declared within a function will be hoisted to the top. Consequently, if there exists a variable with an identical name in the global scope, it will become concealed within the function. For example:

```
var a = 10;

function fn() {
  console.log(a);     // → undefined
  var a = 20;
```

```
  console.log(a);      // → 20
}
fn();
```

So, when looking at the first line of this function, you might think it'll log 10 and 20. But JavaScript actually processes the code differently:

```
var a = 10;
function fn() {
  var a;
  console.log(a);      // → undefined
  a = 20;
  console.log(a);      // → 20
}
fn();
```

To make sure things go smoothly and we don't run into any surprises, ES2015 came up with a solution: the let keyword for declaring variables. With let, variables still get hoisted, but now they're like reminders. They'll give us a heads-up if we try to use a variable that hasn't been declared, preventing any unexpected hiccups:

```
function fn() {
    console.log(a);    // → undefined
    console.log(b);    // → ReferenceError: b is not defined

    var a = 20;
    let b = 20

    console.log(a);
}
fn();
```

So with var, when you try to get hold of a variable before it's declared, you'll get undefined as a response. On the other hand, if you attempt the same thing with let, you'll get an error message. As with let, if you try to use a const or class before declaring them, you'll get a ReferenceError thrown your way.

Temporal dead zone (TDZ) is a term dubbed by the JavaScript community to describe why it's not possible to access let and const before they are declared. let and const are both hoisted similarly to var and function declarations, but there is a time span between entering the scope and being declared in which they cannot be accessed. This period is the temporal dead zone.

Any attempt to access variables while they are in TDZ causes a ReferenceError. Once execution reaches the declaration, the variable in TDZ is removed, and they are allowed to be accessed. The TDZ exists to help us find bugs in our code. Trying to access a variable before declaring it is rarely intentional.

The Lifespan of Variables

 The lifespan of variables within a function spans the duration of the function's execution. Once a function concludes its execution, all local variables within it are automatically cleared. In contrast, global variables remain in memory until the program/webpage is closed.

It's important to remember that TDZ applies only to the code block in which the variable is declared. Attempting to access a variable outside its scope does not throw an error because the variable is not in TDZ:

```javascript
console.log(a);      // → undefined
{
  console.log(a);      // → ReferenceError
  let a = 10;
}
var a = 20;
```

Function Hoisting

Similar to variables, function declarations are hoisted to the top of their containing scope. But they are hoisted entirely, including both the name and the function body. This means you can call a function declared using function before the actual declaration in the code:

```javascript
fn1();      // → Hello!
function fn1() {
 console.log("Hello!");
}
```

Function expressions, on the other hand, are not hoisted in the same way. Only the variable declaration is hoisted, and the function assignment occurs at the point where the variable is declared:

```javascript
fn2();      // → TypeError: fn2 is not a function
var fn2 = function() {
 console.log("Hello!");
};
```

In this case, the variable fn2 is initially assigned undefined, so you can't call it as a function until the assignment is made.

So remember, it's best to declare variables at the top of the scope they belong to. That way, you'll steer clear of any confusion down the road. Additionally, try to get into the habit of using let and const instead of var because they help prevent potential problems like variable hoisting and accidental variable redeclaration.

Further Reading

JavaScript hoisting
> https://developer.mozilla.org/en-US/docs/Glossary/Hoisting

The var statement
> https://developer.mozilla.org/en-US/docs/Web/JavaScript/Reference/Statements/var

The let declaration
> https://developer.mozilla.org/en-US/docs/Web/JavaScript/Reference/Statements/let

The const declaration
> https://developer.mozilla.org/en-US/docs/Web/JavaScript/Reference/Statements/const

The Usurper

the_usurper/the_usurper.js

```javascript
// Calculate the area of a rectangle
function calculateArea(length, width) {
  return length * width;
}

// Calculate the area of a square
function calculateArea(length) {
  return length * length;
}

console.log(calculateArea(4, 6));
```

Guess the Output

 Try to guess what the output is before moving to the next page.

You might have expected the first function, which accepts two arguments, to be executed, but the second function is executed resulting in the following output:

16

Discussion

JavaScript doesn't support *function overloading* like you might be used to in other languages. Function overloading means having multiple functions with the same name but different parameter lists, and the right function gets called based on the arguments you provide.

In JavaScript, if you define multiple functions with the same name, the last one you define will replace the previous functions. But, there's a workaround. You just need to be a little creative.

Instead of having separate functions, you can write a single function and then check the types and number of arguments inside it. Based on what you find, you can make your function behave differently. It's a bit different from traditional function overloading, but it gets the job done in JavaScript:

```
the_usurper/the_usurper_ex1.js
function calculateArea(length, width) {
  if (width === undefined) {
    // Calculate area of a square
    return length * length;
  } else {
    // Calculate area of a rectangle
    return length * width;
  }
}

console.log(calculateArea(5));      // → 25 (Area of a square)
console.log(calculateArea(4, 6));   // → 24 (Area of a rectangle)
```

In this example, we have a function that can calculate the area of both squares and rectangles. Here's how it works: if we call the function with just one argument, the second argument will have a value of undefined. So, it squares the length value and gives us the area we want.

But, if we decide to pass two arguments, the function realizes that we're dealing with a rectangle. So, it multiplies the length and width values together and we get the area of that rectangle.

This trick allows us to have a single function that does all the work. Now, it's worth mentioning that with the introduction of ECMAScript 2015 (ES6), JavaScript got some new tricks up its sleeve. Default function parameters and the rest parameter syntax can help us handle different numbers of arguments with more flexibility.

It's good to keep in mind that true function overloading based on parameter types isn't something JavaScript has built-in. But hey, we can still achieve some pretty cool stuff with what JavaScript offers!

Further Reading

Function overloading

https://en.wikipedia.org/wiki/Function_overloading

Default parameters

https://developer.mozilla.org/en-US/docs/Web/JavaScript/Reference/Functions/Default_parameters

Rest parameters

https://developer.mozilla.org/en-US/docs/Web/JavaScript/Reference/Functions/rest_parameters

The Mathemagician

the_mathemagician/the_mathemagician.js

```javascript
const largeNumber = Math.pow(10, 16);
const smallNumber = 1;

console.log(largeNumber + smallNumber);
```

Guess the Output

 Try to guess what the output is before moving to the next page.

You might have expected the output to be 10000000000000001, but this code will actually log:

```
10000000000000000
```

Discussion

In JavaScript, the Math.pow() function can be used to raise a number to a specified power. In this case, the code Math.pow(10, 16) calculates the result of raising the number 10 to the power of 16, resulting in 10000000000000000. But why does the sum of 10000000000000000 and 1 equal 10000000000000000?

JavaScript does have some limitations when it comes to representing very large numbers accurately. The limitation is due to the way numbers are stored and the precision of the data type used in JavaScript. The Number type has a specific range where it works best. It can handle integers between -9007199254740991 and 9007199254740991 perfectly without losing any precision.

But if you happen to use an integer outside of this range, there's a chance that it won't be represented accurately. This issue is known as *loss of precision* when dealing with large numbers in JavaScript. Here's another example you can try:

```
console.log(9999999999999999);    // → 10000000000000000
```

JavaScript has got you covered with a couple of handy constants that make it easy to get the maximum and minimum safe integers. Just use the Number.MAX_SAFE_INTEGER constant to get the largest safe integer and the Number.MIN_SAFE_INTEGER constant to grab the smallest safe integer:

```
console.log(Number.MIN_SAFE_INTEGER);    // → -9007199254740991
console.log(Number.MAX_SAFE_INTEGER);    // → 9007199254740991
```

Previously, to handle very large numbers with precision, JavaScript developers had to use external libraries like BigInt.js[2] or BigNumber.js.[3] Fortunately, ECMAScript 2020 (the standardized specification for JavaScript) came to the rescue with a fantastic solution called BigInt. Creating a BigInt is easy: simply append the letter n to the end of an integer, like this:

```
console.log(9999999999999999n);    // → 9999999999999999n
```

---

2. https://github.com/TimothyMeadows/bigintjs
3. https://mikemcl.github.io/bignumber.js/

Or, you can use the BigInt() constructor:

```
BigInt("9999999999999999");    // → 9999999999999999n
```

So, to fix the code in this puzzle, we can write:

```
const largeNumber = BigInt("10000000000000000");
const smallNumber = BigInt("1");;

console.log(largeNumber + smallNumber);
// → 10000000000000001n
```

You might be curious about why we're also converting the smallNumber to a BigInt. To maintain the integrity of the data and avoid potential loss of information, mixed operations between BigInts and Numbers are not permitted. The reason behind this restriction is that the resulting value may not be accurately representable by either BigInt or Number data types.

Let's take a look at the following example to better understand this:

```
10000000000000000n + 0.5;
// → TypeError: Cannot mix BigInt and other types, use explicit conversions
```

Converting a Number with a fractional part to a BigInt may not yield an accurate representation, just as converting a BigInt larger than 2^{53} to a Number may also result in loss of precision.

When performing arithmetic computations involving both BigInt and Number values, you have to choose the domain in which the operation should take place. Convert either of the operands by using the functions Number() or BigInt():

```
// convert the Number to a BigInt
BigInt(5) + 5n;    // → 10n

// or convert the BigInt to a Number
5 + Number(5n);    // → 10
```

There are some subtle differences between a Number and a BigInt. You can use all arithmetic operators on a BigInt except for the unary plus (+) operator:

```
console.log(1n + 2n);    // → 3n
console.log(1n - 2n);    // → -1n
console.log(1n * 2n);    // → 2n
console.log(2n / 1n);    // → 2n
console.log(14n % 10n);  // → 4n
console.log(5n ** 3n);   // → 125n

let x = 1n;
console.log(++x);   // → 2n
console.log(--x);   // → 1n
console.log(-x);    // → -1n
console.log(+x);    // → TypeError: Cannot convert a BigInt value to a Number
```

The unary plus (+) operator is not supported for a reason. Some programs may depend on the fact that the + operator always results in a Number or throws an exception. By not supporting it, JavaScript ensures that your code remains reliable and consistent.

When you use arithmetic operators with BigInt operands, you would expect them to return a BigInt value. So, when it comes to the division (/) operator, the result is automatically truncated to maintain consistency with this expectation:

```
console.log(12 / 5);     // → 2.4
console.log(12n / 5n);   // → 2n
```

When it comes to comparing a BigInt with a regular number, remember that they are not of the same type. This means you can't use the strict equality operator (===) directly to compare them:

```
console.log(1n === 1);   // → false
console.log(typeof 1n);  // → bigint
console.log(typeof 1);   // → number
```

However, you do have the option to use the equality operator (==), which automatically converts the types of its operands (known as *type coercion*) before comparing them:

```
console.log(10n == 10);  // → true
```

It's worth mentioning that you should also avoid passing a BigInt as an argument to built-in JavaScript functions and APIs that specifically require a Number. Doing so will trigger a TypeError, as in this example:

```
Math.min(5n, 10n, 15n);  // → TypeError
```

So, you should use the Number data type when dealing with regular numeric values that fall within the range of -9007199254740991 and 9007199254740991, which is suitable for most everyday calculations.

On the other hand, you should opt for the BigInt data type when working with exceptionally large integer values that exceed the safe limits of the Number type, as BigInt allows for arbitrary precision arithmetic and can accurately represent and manipulate integers of any size, albeit at a potential performance cost.

Further Reading

The BigInt value
> developer.mozilla.org/en-US/docs/Web/JavaScript/Reference/Global_Objects/BigInt

Mortal Koncatenation

mortal_koncatenation/mortal_koncatenation.js

```
const femaleMKCharacters = [
  "Sonya Blade",
  "Sindel",
  "Cassie Cage",
  "Sheeva"
];

const maleMKCharacters = [
  "Scorpion",
  "Sub-Zero",
  "Raiden",
  "Johnny Cage"
];

const MKCharacters = femaleMKCharacters + maleMKCharacters;

console.log(MKCharacters);
```

Guess the Output

 Try to guess what the output is before moving to the next page.

You might have anticipated that the output would be a merged array, but this code will actually output:

```
Sonya Blade,Sindel,Cassie Cage,SheevaScorpion,Sub-Zero,Raiden,Johnny Cage
```

Discussion

This JavaScript code defines two arrays: femaleMKCharacters and maleMKCharacters. The femaleMKCharacters array contains the names of female characters from the Mortal Kombat video game series, whereas the maleMKCharacters array contains the names of male characters from the same game.

The puzzle then attempts to combine two arrays into one big array using the + operator. But here's the problem: when you use the + operator with arrays in JavaScript, it doesn't merge them as you might expect. Instead, it treats them as strings and does string concatenation. So, the end result is that MKCharacters becomes a single string that smashes the two arrays together as if they were strings.

Fortunately, there are multiple ways to combine two arrays. Here are a few common approaches:

1. concat(): A quick way to combine two arrays is by using concat(). This method creates a new array that includes the elements from both arrays:

    mortal_koncatenation/mortal_koncatenation_ex1.js
    ```
    const array1 = [1, 2, 3];
    const array2 = [4, 5, 6];
    const combinedArray = array1.concat(array2);

    console.log(combinedArray);     // → [1, 2, 3, 4, 5, 6]
    ```

    You can also use concat() when you have a variable number of arrays to concatenate or if you need to concatenate arrays dynamically based on certain conditions.

2. Spread Operator: The spread operator (...) is a newer feature introduced in ECMAScript 2015 (ES6) that provides a concise way to combine arrays. It unpacks the elements of each array and creates a new array with all the elements:

    mortal_koncatenation/mortal_koncatenation_ex2.js
    ```
    const array1 = [1, 2, 3];
    const array2 = [4, 5, 6];
    const combinedArray = [...array1, ...array2];

    console.log(combinedArray);     // → [1, 2, 3, 4, 5, 6]
    ```

Compared to concat(), the spread operator is more readable, especially when you only need to combine a couple of arrays.

3. push() or unshift(): You can also use array manipulation methods like push() or unshift() to merge arrays:

mortal_koncatenation/mortal_koncatenation_ex3-1.js
```
const array1 = [1, 2, 3];
const array2 = [4, 5, 6];

// Combining arrays using push()
array1.push(...array2);
console.log(array1);     // → [1, 2, 3, 4, 5, 6]
```

mortal_koncatenation/mortal_koncatenation_ex3-2.js
```
const array1 = [1, 2, 3];
const array2 = [4, 5, 6];

// Combining arrays using unshift()
array1.unshift(...array2);
console.log(array1);     // → [4, 5, 6, 1, 2, 3]
```

The push() method appends the elements of the second array to the end of the first array, while unshift() adds them to the beginning.

4. splice(): If you want to insert the elements of an array into another array at a specific index, you can use the splice() method:

mortal_koncatenation/mortal_koncatenation_ex4.js
```
const array1 = [1, 2, 3];
const array2 = [4, 5, 6];

// Assuming you want to add array2 to array1 at index 2
const insertIndex = 2;

// Using splice() to insert the elements of array2 into array1
array1.splice(insertIndex, 0, ...array2);

console.log(array1);     // → [1, 2, 4, 5, 6, 3]
```

These are some of the common ways to combine two arrays in JavaScript. Keep in mind that concat() and the spread operator do not alter the existing arrays; instead, they return a new array. On the contrary, push(), unshift(), and splice() modify the contents of the array they are applied to. Choose the method that best suits your specific requirements and coding style.

Further Reading

A complete list of available array methods

https://developer.mozilla.org/en-US/docs/Web/JavaScript/Reference/Global_Objects/ Array#instance_methods

Offbeat Identifierz

offbeat_identifierz/offbeat_identifierz.js

```
let シ = "\u2663";

console.log(シ);
```

Guess the Output

 Try to guess what the output is before moving to the next page.

This code will output:

♣

Discussion

You might be surprised that シ (which is a Japanese character called "shi") is a valid identifier in JavaScript and that "\u2663" converts to a single character. But, in JavaScript, you can use a wide range of Unicode characters as identifiers. Surprisingly, not many developers know about this cool feature.

And that's not all! You can also make use of Unicode escape sequences to rescue yourself from special characters that hold meaning in your code or to display those tricky-to-type characters, including foreign language characters, mathematical symbols, and even emojis.

Since ECMAScript 2015, you can use most Unicode characters as an identifier in JavaScript. According to the ECMAScript specification, JavaScript allows the use of Unicode characters in identifiers for variables, functions, classes, and other language constructs.

Here's a function with an identifier in the Persian language:

offbeat_identifierz/offbeat_identifierz_ex1.js
```
function سلام() {
  return "Hello";
}

سلام();    // → "Hello"
```

Avoid Copy-Pasting from PDF

If you want to try this code, don't just copy-paste it from the PDF because it might not grab all those fancy Unicode characters. Instead, click on the small gray box located above the code segment to retrieve the JavaScript file.

However, there are some restrictions on the characters that can be used:

- The first character of an identifier must be a Unicode letter (category L), an underscore (_), a dollar sign ($), or a Unicode escape sequence

- Subsequent characters can be letters, digits, underscores, dollar signs, or Unicode escape sequences (we'll talk about Unicode escape sequences shortly)

- Reserved words and keywords cannot be used as identifiers (for a list of reserved words, visit MDN)[4]

Using Unicode characters as an identifier can be quite convenient, but it's important to consider how it can potentially complicate the lives of your fellow programmers. So, I recommend sticking to the tried-and-true ASCII for the sake of everyone's convenience.

Now, let's go back to our puzzle, where we assigned \u2663 to a constant. The visuals displayed on computers represent binary information comprising sequences of ones and zeros. Character encoding steps in to make sense of these binary bits and turn them into actual characters we understand.

To pull this off, each character gets linked to a special number, known as a code point. So, for instance, take the black club suit character (♣)—it's linked to the code point U+2663. When a character gets tied to a specific code point, it's called an encoded character.

In JavaScript, you have the ability to directly use the code point of a character by adding \u before the code point, as in this example:

```
console.log("\u2663");    // → ♣
```

When you write a string like that, you're generating what's referred to as a *Unicode escape sequence*. Unicode escape sequences are particularly useful when you want to use escape characters with special meanings in your code or display those hard-to-type characters, like foreign language characters, mathematical symbols, or even emojis.

Further Reading

Valid JavaScript variable names in ES2015
    mathiasbynens.be/notes/javascript-identifiers-es6

Information about the Unicode character シ (U+30B7)
    compart.com/en/unicode/U+30B7

Identifier definition
    developer.mozilla.org/en-US/docs/Glossary/Identifier

Unicode character properties
    unicode.org/versions/Unicode15.0.0/ch04.pdf

---

4.   https://developer.mozilla.org/en-US/docs/Web/JavaScript/Reference/Lexical_grammar#reserved_words

The Fun-ction

```javascript
!function() {
  const name = "john";
  const age = 20;
}();

const capitalizedName = name[0].toUpperCase() + name.slice(1);

console.log(capitalizedName);
```

Guess the Output

Try to guess what the output is before moving to the next page.

You might have expected the output to be the capitalized name "John", but this code will actually log:

```
TypeError: Cannot read properties of undefined
```

Discussion

The problem in this code is that name has what we call *function scope*, meaning it's accessible only within that function. So, if you attempt to use the value of name out of the function, you'll encounter a reference error because name is undefined in the outer scope.

The function in this puzzle is known as an *immediately invoked function expression* (IIFE). It's a handy design pattern that lets you execute a function right after defining it. The best part is that it helps you create a separate scope for your variables so you don't mess up the global namespace.

When it comes to defining IIFEs, there's actually more than one way to do it. Let's dive in and explore the various forms of syntax you can use for IIFEs:

1. Traditional Parentheses Enclosure:

```
(function() {
  // function body
})();
```

In this form, the IIFE is enclosed within parentheses. The magic happens when we define the function inside those parentheses and then immediately invoke it by adding another set of parentheses at the end. You can also write this form with an arrow function, like this:

```
(() => {
  // function body
})();
```

This syntax is widely used and considered the standard way of writing IIFEs.

2. Unary Operator Enclosure:

```
!function() {
  // function body
}();
```

In this form, the IIFE is preceded by the Logical NOT (!) operator. We define the function after the operator and go ahead and immediately invoke it with (). Now, here's the fun part: you can actually use other unary operators like +, -, or ~ if you feel like it. The reason we use an operator is to make sure that the function is treated like an expression. It's a shorthand way of saying, "Execute this function immediately."

3. Grouping Operator Enclosure:

```
(function() {
  // function body
}());
```

This form is similar to the traditional parentheses enclosure, but the outer set of parentheses is placed around the whole IIFE expression. We define the function inside the parentheses, and the inner pair of parentheses () immediately invokes it.

4. Function Declaration Enclosure:

```
(function namedIIFE() {
  // function body
})();
```

In this form, the IIFE is a named function expression enclosed within parentheses. Why do we give it a name, you ask? Well, it's all about making life easier when we're checking stack traces or using some fancy recursion inside the function. We define the function inside parentheses and immediately invoke it with ().

So, we have these different forms of IIFE that give us some flexibility when it comes to writing self-executing functions. It's totally up to you—your own personal preference and coding style—to choose which syntax floats your boat. However, if you're collaborating in a team, you might prefer using the traditional parentheses enclosure since more developers are familiar with its syntax.

Further Reading

IIFE definition
> https://developer.mozilla.org/en-US/docs/Glossary/IIFE

Scope definition
> https://developer.mozilla.org/en-US/docs/Glossary/Scope

How Long Is a Pirate Flag?

pirate_flag/pirate_flag.js

```
// Happy Flag Day!

const flag = "
```

```
";

console.log(flag.length);
```

Guess the Output

!   Try to guess what the output is before moving to the next page.

You might have anticipated that the output would be 1, but this code will actually output:

4

Discussion

The length of emojis may not be what you expect. In JavaScript, some characters and emojis are formed by multiple code units, which can lead to unexpected results when using the length property. The Pirate Flag emoji is called an Emoji ZWJ Sequence, and it's made up of two separate emojis:

When a zero-width joiner (ZWJ) is placed between these emojis, they are displayed as a connected sequence on platforms that support it. The ZWJ itself is a non-printing character that enables this connected display. The length of the Pirate Flag emoji is 4 because the length property counts the code unit of each independent emoji as well as the ZWJ required to connect them.

In the realm of JavaScript, the sequence of code points \uD83C\uDFF4 represents the black flag emoji, while the solitary skull emoji is denoted by the code point \u2620. When combined, including the ZWJ in between, their collective length totals four characters.

Variation Selectors Extend Emoji/Character Length

Unicode variation selectors are used to indicate specific variations or alternate representations of a character or emoji, typically for purposes like skin tone modifications or presentation style variations.

In many cases, a character can be represented without a variation selector, and the default representation will be used. The Pirate Flag emoji might include a variation selector, which would increase the emoji's length from 4 to 5 characters. For more information on the variation selector, please see the "Further Reading" section.

To tackle this issue, we have the Internationalization API. It provides a handy method called Segmenter() that helps you segment strings properly, taking into account the intended segmentation rules of various languages and scripts:

pirate_flag/pirate_flag_ex1.js
```
// The correct way to calculate the length of emojis

function getLength(str) {
 return [...new Intl.Segmenter().segment(str)].length;
}

getLength("🏴‍☠️");    // → 1
```

The Intl.Segmenter() constructor is a handy tool that allows you to break down a string based on a specific locale and granularity. In this case, we're keeping it simple by using the default settings, so you just call the method without any arguments. Just remember that because Intl.Segmenter() is a constructor, you'll want to use it with the new keyword.

When you call Intl.Segmenter(), it gives you back an object that has a segment() method. This method takes a string as its input and does exactly what it sounds like—it divides the string into those segments that make sense to humans. Because the result is an iterator, you can make life easier by using the spread syntax, which is those three dots in a row (...). This syntax allows you to quickly transform the iterator into an array and obtain its length.

If the code seems a bit confusing, we've got an alternative version for you to use:

pirate_flag/pirate_flag_ex2.js
```
function getLength(str) {
  // Create a an instance of segmenter
  const Segmenter = new Intl.Segmenter();

  // Segment the string
  const segment = Segmenter.segment(str);

  // Convert it into an array
  const arr = Array.from(segment);

  // Return the number of characters
  return arr.length;
}
```

This version of the code performs the same operations as the first one.

The Internationalization API is really clever when it comes to counting ZWJ emojis. It treats them as a single character, which makes things much easier for us. Whenever you need to get the length of a string that may contain emojis or Unicode characters, consider using the Intl.Segmenter() method.

Further Reading

The pirate flag emoji
> http://www.unicode.org/L2/L2018/18059-pirate-flag.pdf

General variation sequences FAQ
http://unicode.org/faq/vs.html

The Intl.Segmenter object
https://developer.mozilla.org/en-US/docs/Web/JavaScript/Reference/Global_Objects/Intl/Segmenter

The Internationalization API
https://developer.mozilla.org/en-US/docs/Web/JavaScript/Reference/Global_Objects/Intl

The zero-width joiner
https://en.wikipedia.org/wiki/Zero-width_joiner

What's This?

whats_this/whats_this.js

```
let key = 2049;

(function() {
  "use strict";
  console.log(this.key);
})();
```

Guess the Output

 Try to guess what the output is before moving to the next page.

This code will output:

```
TypeError: Cannot read properties of undefined
```

Discussion

The this keyword in JavaScript can be a bit tricky because its value depends on where the code is running and how it's being used. If you run the code outside of any specific function or object, this refers to the global object. In a web browser, the global object is usually window, and in Node.js, it's global. So, if you run console.log(this) in a web browser's console, you'll see the value of window printed out.

But here's the interesting part: the value of this can change depending on the context. If you're inside a function that is not part of an object, then this might be different. In strict mode, it'll be undefined, and in non-strict mode, it'll be the global object again:

whats_this/whats_this_ex1.js
```
(function() {
  "use strict";
  console.log(this);    // → undefined
})();

(function() {
  console.log(this);    // → Window {...}
})();
```

In this puzzle, we are attempting to read the key property of undefined inside an immediately invoked function expression (IIFE). Remember, an IIFE is a function that is executed immediately after its creation. Since undefined lacks properties, the code generates an error.

Notice the "use strict" expression at the top of the function. This line tells the JavaScript engine to enable strict mode in the function. Strict mode is a way to opt into a stricter set of rules and behaviors enforced by the JavaScript engine, which helps to catch common coding mistakes and "unsafe" actions, ultimately leading to more robust and maintainable code.

Without "use strict", the function logs undefined instead of throwing an error:

whats_this/whats_this_ex2.js
```
let key = 2049;

(function() {
  console.log(this.key);    // → undefined
})();
```

Now, if we used this inside an object's method, it would point to the object itself. So, if you call a method of an object like object.method(), then this will be the object of that method:

```
whats_this/whats_this_ex3.js
const user = {
  firstName: "Mikasa",
  lastName: "Ackerman",
  getFullname() {
    return `${this.firstName} ${this.lastName}`;
  }
};

console.log(user.getFullname());    // → Mikasa Ackerman
```

If you use the new keyword to create objects using a constructor function, this will refer to the newly created object:

```
whats_this/whats_this_ex4.js
function Book(name, year) {
  this.name = name;
  this.year = year;
  this.getBookInfo = () => {
    return `${this.name} (${this.year})`;
  }
}

const book1 = new Book("Death by Black Hole", 2006);
book1.getBookInfo();    // → Death by Black Hole (2006)
```

And finally, if you explicitly set the value of this using methods like call(), apply(), or bind(), it will refer to the object you pass as the first argument:

```
whats_this/whats_this_ex5.js
function describeMeal() {
  return `A ${this.dish} usually has about ${this.calories} calories.`;
}

const meal = {
  dish: "salad",
  calories: "300",
};

console.log(describeMeal.call(meal));
// → A salad usually has about 300 calories.
```

So, running console.log(this) will give you different outputs depending on where the code is running and how it's being used. Keep in mind that if you use this to access the global object, it could make your code less portable. Every JavaScript environment has its own object model and different ways to reach the global object. In a web browser, you can access the global object using window, self, this, or frames. It's pretty flexible!

For example, window.alert('Hello') accesses the global object (window) and invokes the alert method. Additionally, you can access the global object directly without using the window prefix. For example, alert('Hello') would work as well.

In Node.js, however, properties like window and self don't exist, and you must use global instead. In Web Workers, only self is available. These different ways of referencing the global object have made it tough to write portable JavaScript code that works in multiple environments.

Fortunately, ECMAScript fixed this issue in ES2020 by introducing a standard property called globalThis that's available in all environments:

whats_this/whats_this_ex6.js

```
// Browser environment
console.log(globalThis);    // → Window {...}

// Node.js environment
console.log(globalThis);    // → <ref *1> Object [global] {...}

// Web worker environment
console.log(globalThis);    // → DedicatedWorkerGlobalScope {...}
```

By using globalThis, your code will work effortlessly in both window and non-window contexts without the need for extra checks.

When you're unsure about the environment in which your code will be utilized or if you want to ensure its compatibility across different environments, the globalThis property becomes incredibly useful. Keep in mind that older browsers may require a polyfill. A polyfill is a piece of code that provides modern JavaScript features to older web browsers that lack native support for those features.

On the other hand, if you're confident about the specific environment in which your code will be used, you can rely on existing methods to reference the global object of that environment. This way, you can avoid the hassle of including a polyfill.

Further Reading

What is globalThis, and why should you start using it?
https://blog.logrocket.com/what-is-globalthis-why-use-it/

The globalThis global property
https://developer.mozilla.org/en-US/docs/Web/JavaScript/Reference/Global_Objects/globalThis

The Flat Earth Society

the_flat_earth_society/the_flat_earth_society.js

```javascript
const nestedArray = ["apple", ["blueberry", "blackberry"],
                    ["tangerine", "orange"], "grape"];
const newArr = [].concat.apply([], nestedArray);

console.log(newArr);
```

Guess the Output

 Try to guess what the output is before moving to the next page.

This code will output:

```
['apple', 'blueberry', 'blackberry', 'tangerine', 'orange', 'grape']
```

Discussion

This JavaScript code is all about flattening an array of arrays. First, we have an array called nestedArray. It contains four elements: two strings and two sub-arrays. The second line of code does the magic of flattening the array. Here's how it works:

1. [] creates an empty array. This will be the initial value for the concat() method.

2. concat() is a built-in JavaScript array method used to merge two or more arrays together. It takes one or more arrays as arguments and returns a new array containing the elements of all the input arrays combined.

3. apply() is a method that allows you to call a function with a given this value and an array (or an array-like object) as arguments. In this case, we're using it to apply the concat method to the empty array [] while passing the elements of nestedArray as arguments.

So, when you run [].concat.apply([], nestedArray), it essentially takes all the elements from nestedArray and concatenates them into a single, flat array. This is a common technique for flattening nested arrays in JavaScript.

But this doesn't seem like the most elegant solution, does it?

Fortunately, since ES2019, there's this handy method called flat() that allows you to quickly flatten a nested array by collapsing all sub-arrays into a single-dimensional array.

Here's how you can use the flat() method:

the_flat_earth_society/the_flat_earth_society_ex1.js
```js
const nestedArray = ["apple", ["blueberry", "blackberry"],
                    ["tangerine", "orange"], "grape"];
const flattenedArray = nestedArray.flat();

console.log(flattenedArray);
// → ["apple", "blueberry", "blackberry", "tangerine", "orange", "grape"]
```

flat() magically goes through all the levels of nesting and creates a single-dimensional array. But wait, there's more! You can also provide an optional parameter called depth to control how many levels of nesting it will flatten.

By default, depth is set to 1, meaning it flattens just one level, but you can specify a different depth if you want to go deeper. If you set the depth to Infinity, it will flatten all levels, no matter how deep they go:

the_flat_earth_society/the_flat_earth_society_ex2.js

```js
const deeplyNestedArray = ["a", ["b", ["c", ["d", ["e"]]]]];
const flattenedArray = deeplyNestedArray.flat(Infinity);

console.log(flattenedArray);
// → ["a", "b", "c", "d", "e"]
```

Just remember that when you use flat(), it creates a brand new array and leaves the original array untouched. If you don't need the original array anymore, you can directly assign the flattened array to the same variable.

Further Reading

Google's v8 blog
> https://v8.dev/features/array-flat-flatmap

The flat() method
> https://developer.mozilla.org/en-US/docs/Web/JavaScript/Reference/Global_Objects/Array/flat

The apply() method
> https://developer.mozilla.org/en-US/docs/Web/JavaScript/Reference/Global_Objects/Function/apply

Casting Spells with 1s and 0s

casting_spells/casting_spells.js

```
const x = ~~(7.9);

console.log(x);
```

Guess the Output

 Try to guess what the output is before moving to the next page.

This code will output:

```
7
```

Discussion

The tilde (~) symbol in JavaScript is known as the bitwise NOT operator. It takes the binary representation of a number and flips all the bits, resulting in a new number. Now, the thing is, bitwise operators in JavaScript work with integers, not floating-point numbers.

So, when you have the expression ~~(7.9), JavaScript automatically converts the floating-point number 7.9 into an integer. In this case, it truncates the decimal part and turns it into the integer 7. Now, let's see what happens when we apply a single bitwise NOT operator: ~(7.9). In binary, 7 is represented as 00000111. The NOT operator flips each bit, so we get 11111000, resulting in 248.

But wait, in this puzzle, we have two bitwise NOT operators. So, the next step for JavaScript is to convert 248 into its binary representation and flip bits. It flips each and every bit of the binary representation. So, 11111000 becomes 00000111 again.

Finally, JavaScript interprets this flipped binary number as an integer, and we get the result: 7. So, that's why the result of the code ~~(7.9) in JavaScript is 7. It's a clever trick to chop off the decimal part of a number. Using this technique, you can shave off a few bytes in your code when converting numbers to integers. Just remember, though, that it's considered a hacky way because it'll behave unexpectedly if you're working with numbers beyond the range of 32-bit signed integers.

For example:

```
console.log(~~2147500000.5);    // → -2147467296
```

So, the double tilde trick works well if your number is within a moderate range and not too large or too small. But, if you happen to be working with a number that's outside the range of -2147483648 to 2147483647, you'd be better off sticking with the trusty built-in functions like Math.floor(), Math.ceil(), or Math.round().

Remember to Add Comments to Your Code

 If you find yourself using a coding technique that's a bit out of the ordinary, it's a great idea to sprinkle in some helpful code comments. Thinking about the future, it's always nice to make things easy for your future self or any fellow developers who might work with your code.

Further Reading

The bitwise NOT (~) operator

https://developer.mozilla.org/en-US/docs/Web/JavaScript/Reference/Operators/Bitwise_NOT

Binary to decimal converter

https://www.rapidtables.com/convert/number/binary-to-decimal.html

Dating with Math

`dating_with_math/dating_with_math.js`

```
const date = new Date;
const x = date % 100;

console.log(x);
```

Guess the Output

 Try to guess what the output is before moving to the next page.

This code will output a number between 0 and 99.

Discussion

In JavaScript, the Date object represents a specific point in time. When you create a new instance of the Date object using the new keyword, it initializes with the current date and time.

Now, what this code does is take that current date and time and divide it by 100. This approach works because when you perform integer math on a new Date object, it is converted into a number like 1687530684418—which is the number of milliseconds that have elapsed since 00:00:00 UTC on 1 January 1970 (Unix epoch). This timestamp is commonly used in programming languages to represent and manipulate dates and times.

But we're not interested in the actual division result. We just want to know the remainder, like when you divide numbers and get a leftover bit. That's where the % symbol, called the *modulo operator*, comes in. When used with a numeric expression, such as x % y, it divides x by y and returns the remainder.

The result will be an integer between 0 and 99 (inclusive). This technique can be useful in scenarios where you need to obtain a number between 0 and a specific number. For example, you might use it to get a number between 0 and 7 by using % 7:

```
new Date % 7
```

The output will vary each time you run the code since it depends on the current date and time when the code is executed.

Keep in mind that it would be technically inaccurate to say that Date % n returns a random number. When called rapidly, it can yield identical or sequential numbers, which doesn't align with the typical understanding of "random numbers" in programming. For example:

```
for (let i = 0; i < 10; i++) {
  console.log(new Date % 7);
}
// → 5
// → 5
// → 5
// → 5
// → 6
// → 6
// → 6
```

```
// → 6
// → 6
// → 6
```

This inaccuracy happens because we're trying to generate a number using the current date. A more reliable approach is to use the Math.random() method:

```
for (let i = 0; i < 10; i++) {
  console.log(Math.floor(Math.random() * 8));
}
// → 4
// → 6
// → 0
// → 6
// → 2
// → 1
// → 3
// → 5
// → 0
// → 2
```

This code generates ten random integers between 0 and 7. Here's how it works: Math.random() produces a random floating-point number between 0 (inclusive) and 1 (exclusive). We use it here as the basis for generating a random integer.

We take the random value and multiply it by 8. This step scales the random value to a range between 0 (inclusive) and 8 (exclusive). So, now we have a random floating-point number between 0 and 7.9999... (inclusive of 0 but not including 8).

Finally, we use the Math.floor() method to round down the random floating-point number to the nearest integer. This effectively removes the decimal part and leaves us with a random integer between 0 and 7 (inclusive). The range includes 0 because Math.floor(0) is still 0, and it includes 7 because Math.floor(7.9999...) rounds down to 7.

So, remember, while you can use new Date % n as a concise approach to obtain a number between zero and a specific value, it's not truly random and may produce identical or sequential numbers when called rapidly.

Further Reading

The Date object

https://developer.mozilla.org/en-US/docs/Web/JavaScript/Reference/Global_Objects/Date

What's the Value of Math?

whats_the_value_of_math/whats_the_value_of_math.js

```
const r = {valueOf:Math.random},
      a = [r*11|0,r*11|0,r*11|0];

console.log(a);
```

Guess the Output

Try to guess what the output is before moving to the next page.

This code generates an array with three random numbers, for instance:

```
[10, 5, 7]
```

Discussion

JavaScript has a handy property called valueOf that automatically gets called when an object needs to be converted to a primitive value. By assigning Math.random to the valueOf property of an object, we can create a custom object that acts like a random number generator.

Usually, you achieve this task like this:

```
const a = [
  Math.random() * 11 | 0,
  Math.random() * 11 | 0,
  Math.random() * 11 | 0
];
```

The built-in Math.random function generates random floating-point numbers between 0 (inclusive) and 1 (exclusive). First, we take a random decimal value generated by Math.random and multiply it by 11. This gives us a random number between 0 and 11, such as 7.599000342813731.

To make things even more interesting, we use the bitwise OR operator (|) on the result. This operator works its magic by removing the decimal part and converting the number into an integer. For example, if we had 7.599000342813731, using | 0 would give us 7. We repeat this process three times to get three random integers between 0 and 10 (inclusive). These random integers are then stored as elements in the array.

We could also assign Math.random to a variable or constant, which comes in handy when we need to call the function multiple times:

```
const r = Math.random,
a = [
  r() * 11 | 0,
  r() * 11 | 0,
  r() * 11 | 0,
];
```

This brain teaser takes advantage of a nifty way to make the code even shorter! By assigning Math.random to the valueOf property of the object r, we're creating a custom object that acts like a random number generator. Whenever JavaScript wants to convert r to a primitive value, it will call the valueOf function, resulting in a random number thanks to the Math.random assignment.

So, the interesting thing to remember from this puzzle is that you can take advantage of the valueOf property to make your own custom object that works like a shortcut for JavaScript methods and functions.

Further Reading

The valueOf() method
    developer.mozilla.org/en-US/docs/Web/JavaScript/Reference/Global_Objects/Object/valueOf

The Math.random() static method
    developer.mozilla.org/en-US/docs/Web/JavaScript/Reference/Global_Objects/Math/random

The bitwise OR (|) operator
    developer.mozilla.org/en-US/docs/Web/JavaScript/Reference/Operators/Bitwise_OR

Netherlands or Holland?

netherlands_or_holland/netherlands_or_holland.js

```javascript
const country = {
  name: "Netherlands"
};

const name = Symbol("name");

country[name] = "Holland";

console.log(country["name"]);
```

Guess the Output

Try to guess what the output is before moving to the next page.

You might have anticipated that the output would be Holland, but this code will actually output Netherlands.

Discussion

This puzzle is about a fascinating JavaScript feature called *Symbol*. Symbols let us define hidden or private properties within objects. Since symbols are unique, they're unlikely to cause conflicts with other properties. They won't show up in for...in loops or Object.keys(), making them suitable for creating properties that are not intended to be accessed by external code.

In this code, we have an object representing a country. The country we're talking about here is the Netherlands, and we store that information in a property called name. Now, things get a bit interesting. We add a symbol to the object. We create the symbol using the Symbol() function and call it name. It's like giving our symbol a special label.

Next, we add a new piece of information to our country object. Using the symbol name as the key, we set a value of Holland. Think of it as adding a hidden note to our country object. We use square brackets to access the property with the symbol key, like country[name].

Now, if we print country[name] to the console, it will show us the value associated with the symbol key name, which is Holland. On the other hand, if we print country["name"] to the console, it will show us the value associated with the regular string key name. We initially set this value to Netherlands, so when we print it, we see Netherlands in the console.

Symbols are useful when we want to create properties that are not easily accessible or visible from the outside. They provide a way to add hidden or private information to objects. Since symbols are unique, we don't have to worry about accidentally overlapping or conflicting with other property names.

Further Reading

Detailed overview of symbols
> https://exploringjs.com/es6/ch_symbols.html

The symbol object
> https://developer.mozilla.org/en-US/docs/Web/JavaScript/Reference/Global_Objects/Symbol

The Permanent Closure

the_permanent_closure/the_permanent_closure.js

```js
function createCounterArray() {
  const counterArray = [];
  for (var i = 0; i < 5; i++) {
    counterArray.push(() => {
      console.log(`Counter: ${i}`);
    });
  }
  return counterArray;
}

const counters = createCounterArray();

counters.forEach(counter => counter());
```

Guess the Output

Try to guess what the output is before moving to the next page.

You might have expected the output to be:

```
Counter: 0
Counter: 1
Counter: 2
Counter: 3
Counter: 4
```

But this code will output:

```
Counter: 5
Counter: 5
Counter: 5
Counter: 5
Counter: 5
```

Discussion

In this puzzle, the intention is to create an array of closure functions, each printing the current value of the variable i. However, when you run this code, you'll get an unexpected result. Instead of printing the values 0, 1, 2, 3, and 4, the code will print the value 5 five times.

This result is because var has function-level scope, not block-level scope. The variable i declared in the for loop is shared across all the closure functions. By the time the functions are called, the for loop has already finished executing, and the final value of i is 5.

A straightforward approach to fix this issue is to use the let keyword instead of var to declare the variable i. Using let will create a new block-scoped variable for each iteration of the loop:

the_permanent_closure/the_permanent_closure_ex1.js
```js
function createCounterArray() {
  const counterArray = [];
  for (let i = 0; i < 5; i++) {
    counterArray.push(() => {
      console.log(`Counter: ${i}`);
    });
  }
  return counterArray;
}

const counters = createCounterArray();

counters.forEach(counter => counter());
```

With this change, each function in the closureArray will capture its own separate value of i, and you'll see the expected output:

```
Counter: 0
Counter: 1
Counter: 2
Counter: 3
Counter: 4
```

Another way to fix this problem is to use an immediately invoked function expression (IIFE) to create a new scope for each iteration of the loop:

the_permanent_closure/the_permanent_closure_ex2.js
```
function createCounterArray() {
  const counterArray = [];
  for (var i = 0; i < 5; i++) {
    ((i) => {
      counterArray.push(() => {
        console.log(`Counter: ${i}`);
      });
    })(i);
  }
  return counterArray;
}

const counters = createCounterArray();

counters.forEach(counter => counter());
```

In this version, we introduce the IIFE ((i) => { ... })(i) to create a new scope for each iteration of the loop. This ensures that each closure function captures its own copy of i with the correct value. Now, when you run the code, it will print the values 0, 1, 2, 3, and 4 as expected.

JavaScript closures are useful because they enable the creation of self-contained and encapsulated functions that can maintain their own local state, even after the parent function that created them has finished executing. But as we've discovered from this puzzle, it's important to be cautious when making them, or else we might end up with surprising outcomes!

Further Reading

Immediately invoked function expressions
> https://developer.mozilla.org/en-US/docs/Glossary/IIFE

The let declaration
> https://developer.mozilla.org/en-US/docs/Web/JavaScript/Reference/Statements/let

Cracking the Color Code

cracking_the_color_code/cracking_the_color_code.js

```js
const canvas = document.createElement("canvas");
const ctx = canvas.getContext("2d");

ctx.fillStyle = "yellow";

console.log(ctx.fillStyle);
```

Guess the Output

 Try to guess what the output is before moving to the next page.

You might have anticipated that the output would be yellow, but this code will actually output:

```
#ffff00
```

Discussion

What happens here is that we create a temporary HTML canvas, and then we get its 2D context. After that, we set a color for the fillStyle property. Now, here's the unexpected part: when we log ctx.fillStyle using console.log(), instead of showing the color we assigned, it actually converts it to its hexadecimal (hex) representation automatically. Here's what each line of the code does:

1. const canvas = document.createElement("canvas"): This line creates a new canvas element, just like preparing a blank piece of paper. It's like saying, "Hey, let's make a fresh canvas to draw on!"

2. const ctx = canvas.getContext("2d"): This line sets up a "context" for drawing on the canvas. Think of it as getting your brushes, paints, and palette ready. We're using a technique called "2D" drawing, which means we'll be working with two-dimensional shapes like lines and curves.

3. ctx.fillStyle = "yellow": This line is like choosing the color you want to use. Here, we're picking "yellow" as our color. So, any shapes we draw will be filled with yellow.

4. console.log(ctx.fillStyle): This line prints out the current fill color we've chosen in the console. It's like checking your palette to see which color you're using before you start painting. But, instead of printing "yellow", JavaScript implicitly converts it to the corresponding hex representation of the color. So, the actual output is #ffff00.

Hexadecimal notation offers a concise and effective method for denoting a diverse spectrum of colors. By converting color names to hex notation, we can specify a color in a way that can be used across different software platforms and devices.

Further Reading

The getContext() method
https://developer.mozilla.org/en-US/docs/Web/API/HTMLCanvasElement/getContext

The fillStyle property
https://developer.mozilla.org/en-US/docs/Web/API/CanvasRenderingContext2D/fillStyle

Waiting in Line

waiting_in_line/waiting_in_line.js

```js
console.log("Start");

setTimeout(() => {
  console.log("Timeout");
}, 0);

Promise.resolve().then(() => {
  console.log("Promise");
});

console.log("End");
```

Guess the Output

 Try to guess what the output is before moving to the next page.

You might have anticipated that the output would be:

```
Start
Timeout
Promise
End
```

But the code will output:

```
Start
End
Promise
Timeout
```

Discussion

Here, we have a mixture of synchronous and asynchronous operations and use console.log() to output different messages at various points in the code. Since the setTimeout() is set to 0 milliseconds, you might expect the messages to appear in the order of "Start", "Timeout", "Promise", and "End". But, the actual output is different because of the event loop and how JavaScript handles asynchronous tasks.

The event loop is an important part of JavaScript that ensures code execution happens in a non-blocking way. It takes care of tasks like managing asynchronous operations, timers, and callbacks.

In this puzzle, we have two asynchronous tasks: a setTimeout and a Promise. The setTimeout() function allows us to schedule a callback function to run after a specific delay. However, even though we set the delay to 0, the callback function isn't immediately executed. Instead, it's added to the event queue, waiting for the event loop to finish executing the current synchronous code before it gets its turn.

After that, we have a Promise.resolve() statement. Promises are a way to handle asynchronous operations in JavaScript. Here, we create a promise using Promise.resolve(), which immediately resolves the promise with a value of undefined. We then attach a .then() method to the promise, which allows us to specify a function to execute once the promise is resolved. In this example, the function logs the message "Promise" to the console.

Unlike setTimeout(), the Promise.resolve().then code is scheduled to run in the next microtask checkpoint, which happens before the event queue is processed.

Now, when both the setTimeout() and the Promise are present in the code, the following sequence of events occurs:

1. The synchronous code is executed.
2. The setTimeout callback is placed in the event queue.
3. The Promise callback is executed immediately.
4. The event loop picks up the setTimeout callback from the event queue and executes it.

It's important to note that even though the delay in the setTimeout() function is set to 0 milliseconds, the actual delay can vary depending on the workload of the JavaScript engine and other factors. This behavior might seem unexpected if you're not familiar with JavaScript's event loop and asynchronous execution.

Further Reading

Introducing asynchronous JavaScript
    developer.mozilla.org/en-US/docs/Learn/JavaScript/Asynchronous/Introducing

The Promise.resolve() static method
    developer.mozilla.org/en-US/docs/Web/JavaScript/Reference/Global_Objects/Promise/resolve

The setTimeout() method
    developer.mozilla.org/en-US/docs/Web/API/setTimeout

Chasing Promises

chasing_promises/chasing_promises.js

```javascript
console.log("Application started");

async function fetchDataFromAPI() {
  console.log("Fetching data from API...");
  await processAPIData();
  console.log("Data fetched successfully");
}

async function processAPIData() {
  console.log("Processing API data...");
}

fetchDataFromAPI();

console.log("Application ended");
```

Guess the Output

Try to guess what the output is before moving to the next page.

You might have expected the output to be:

```
Application started
Application ended
Fetching data from API...
Processing API data...
Data fetched successfully
```

But this code will actually output:

```
Application started
Fetching data from API...
Processing API data...
Application ended
Data fetched successfully
```

Discussion

The await keyword allows you to write asynchronous code in a more linear fashion, making it easier to understand the flow of execution, even when dealing with operations that take time to complete.

First, we have the synchronous console.log("Application started") that simply logs the string "Application started" to the console. Then we have async function fetchDataFromAPI() { ... }, which declares an asynchronous function. Asynchronous functions can use the await keyword to pause their execution while waiting for a promise to resolve.

Inside the function, await processAPIData() uses the await keyword to pause the execution of the fetchDataFromAPI function until the processAPIData function completes its execution. In this case, since processAPIData is an asynchronous function, it returns a promise, and await ensures that the program will wait for that promise to be resolved before proceeding.

To summarize the sequence of events:

- The code starts by logging "Application started".

- The fetchDataFromAPI function is called, which logs "Fetching data from API...", and awaits the completion of the processAPIData function.

- Inside the processAPIData function, "Processing API data..." is logged.

- The script then logs "Application ended", as it is now allowed to continue to execute outside the fetchDataFromAPI function.

- Finally, "Data fetched successfully" is logged.

So, the await keyword is helpful when you have tasks that take time, like talking to a server, and you want to make sure they happen in a smooth sequence. Here, the code waits for fetchDataFromAPI() and processAPIData() to finish their tasks before moving on. As a result, things happen in a different order.

Further Reading

Modern Asynchronous JavaScript
> https://pragprog.com/titles/fkajs/modern-asynchronous-javascript/

The Promise object
> https://developer.mozilla.org/en-US/docs/Web/JavaScript/Reference/Global_Objects/Promise

The await operator
> https://developer.mozilla.org/en-US/docs/Web/JavaScript/Reference/Operators/await

Oo Na Na Na

```
oo_na_na_na/oo_na_na_na.js
let price = 10;
let tax;

const sum = price + tax;

console.log(sum);
```

Guess the Output

 Try to guess what the output is before moving to the next page.

You might have expected the output to be 10, but this code will actually log:

```
NaN
```

Discussion

In this puzzle, the statement const tax; declares a constant variable without assigning any value to it. So, the variable holds a default value of undefined. When trying to add undefined to the value of price, the operation yields NaN (Not-a-Number).

NaN is a special value in JavaScript that represents the result of an invalid or undefined mathematical operation. You may encounter NaN when doing math operations that don't produce a meaningful numeric value, like trying to divide zero by zero or taking the square root of a negative number.

Here are some JavaScript operations that would result in NaN:

1. When dividing a zero by zero

    ```
    0 / 0;     // → NaN
    ```

2. Attempting to convert a non-numeric string to a number

    ```
    Number("hello");     // → NaN
    ```

3. Parsing an invalid floating-point notation

    ```
    parseFloat("abc");     // → NaN
    ```

4. Performing a mathematical operation involving NaN

    ```
    NaN + 5;     // → NaN
    ```

5. Using an undefined variable in a math operation

    ```
    let x;
    x + 10;     // → NaN
    ```

6. Taking the square root of a negative number

    ```
    Math.sqrt(-9);     // → NaN
    ```

7. Performing certain mathematical operations with Infinity

    ```
    Infinity - Infinity;     // → NaN
    ```

These operations all result in NaN because they involve operations that don't produce meaningful numeric results according to JavaScript's specifications.

Now, here's the tricky part. You can't use the strict equality operator to check if the result of an operation is NaN:

```
oo_na_na_na/oo_na_na_na_ex1.js
let price = 10;
let tax;

const sum = price + tax;

if (sum === NaN) {
  // This won't be excecuted
  console.error("tax or price is undefined");
}
```

The if statement in this code won't be executed even though sum has a value of NaN. When you compare NaN with NaN using the code NaN === NaN, you might expect it to be true, right? I mean, NaN is NaN, so they should be equal. But that's not how JavaScript sees it. In JavaScript, NaN is considered to be "unordered" or "not equal to" anything, including NaN itself.

This is a deliberate design choice in JavaScript and the IEEE 754 standard. The rationale behind this behavior is that NaN represents an undefined or indeterminate value, so it cannot be compared with any other value, including another NaN.

To check if something is NaN in JavaScript, you can use the isNaN() function. For example, isNaN(NaN) would give you true because, well, it is indeed not a number:

```
oo_na_na_na/oo_na_na_na_ex2.js
let price = 10;
let tax;

const sum = price + tax;

if (isNaN(sum)) {
  console.error("tax or price is undefined");
}

// → tax or price is undefined
```

Remember, NaN is a strange beast in JavaScript that doesn't play by the usual rules. It's not equal to anything, not even itself!

Further Reading

The NaN global property
> https://developer.mozilla.org/en-US/docs/Web/JavaScript/Reference/Global_Objects/NaN

Overview of the NaN data type
> https://en.wikipedia.org/wiki/NaN

Hexorcism

hexorcism/Hexorcism.js
```javascript
const hex = "0x1E";

console.log(hex - 0);
```

Guess the Output

 Try to guess what the output is before moving to the next page.

You might have anticipated that the output would be NaN since "0x1E" is a string, but this code will actually output:

30

Discussion

This JavaScript code outputs 30 because of the way JavaScript handles arithmetic operations and type conversions. The "0x" part is a prefix used in JavaScript to indicate that a number is in hexadecimal format. Hexadecimal numbers use a base-16 system instead of the usual base-10 (decimal) system we're more familiar with.

So, "0x" is just a way of saying that we're dealing with a hexadecimal number. When you use the - 0 operation, JavaScript tries to convert the string "0x1E" into a number. JavaScript is clever when it comes to math with strings and numbers. If it can, it will convert a string into a number before performing a mathematical operation.

In this case, JavaScript recognizes that the "0x" at the beginning is a sign that the following characters "1E" represent a hexadecimal number. After recognizing that "0x1E" is a hexadecimal number, JavaScript converts it to its decimal equivalent, which is 30. Then, it performs the subtraction operation 30 - 0, resulting in the final value of 30.

JavaScript offers several ways to convert a hexadecimal number into its decimal equivalent. One commonly used method is by using parseInt(). So, if you're looking for a more explicit approach, you can give parseInt() a try. For example, let's say we have a hexadecimal number: B2F. To convert it to decimal, you can use the following code:

hexorcism/Hexorcism_ex1.js
```
const hexNumber = "B2F";
const decimalNumber = parseInt(hexNumber, 16);

console.log(decimalNumber);    // → 2863
```

In this method, we pass 16 as the second argument to parseInt(), indicating that the input is in base 16 (hexadecimal). Another option is to utilize the Number() constructor. Here's how you can do it:

hexorcism/Hexorcism_ex2.js
```
const hexNumber = "B2F";
const decimalNumber = Number(`0x${hexNumber}`);

console.log(decimalNumber);    // → 2863
```

In this approach, we use the Number() constructor and prefix the hexadecimal number with "0x". This prefix indicates to the constructor that it's dealing with a hexadecimal number and performs the conversion accordingly.

In general, if you're dealing specifically with converting hexadecimal strings to decimal integers, using parseInt() with the specified base (16) is a more explicit choice. Also, remember that JavaScript has limitations when dealing with very large or very small numbers due to the precision of the data type used in JavaScript (see Puzzle 3, The Mathemagician, on page 13). For example:

hexorcism/Hexorcism_ex3.js

```javascript
const hexNumber = "2386F26FC0FFFF";    // equivalent to 9999999999999999
const decimalNumber = parseInt(hexNumber, 16);

console.log(decimalNumber);     // → 10000000000000000
```

The hexadecimal value in this code is equivalent to 9999999999999999, but JavaScript is unable to accurately represent this value. As a result, it displays 10000000000000000 when printed to the console. In such cases, you'll need to use additional libraries or techniques to handle arbitrary precision arithmetic.

Converting Binary and Octal

If you ever need to convert a binary number or an octal number in JavaScript, you can take advantage of the trick you learned in this teaser. Just remember to add either 0b for binary or 0o for octal in front of the number, and you'll get the decimal equivalent. Let me show you an example:

```javascript
const binaryNumber = "0111";
console.log("0b"+binaryNumber-0);    // → 7
```

In this code snippet, we're converting the binary value 0111 to its decimal representation, which is 7.

Further Reading

Overview of the hexadecimal numeral system
en.wikipedia.org/wiki/Hexadecimal

The parseInt() function
developer.mozilla.org/en-US/docs/Web/JavaScript/Reference/Global_Objects/parseInt

The Number() constructor
developer.mozilla.org/en-US/docs/Web/JavaScript/Reference/Global_Objects/Number/Number

The Arrayist

the_arrayist/the_arrayist.js

```
const f = (n) => [...Array(n)].map((_, i) => i + 1);

console.log(f(20));
```

Guess the Output

 Try to guess what the output is before moving to the next page.

This code will output:

```
[1, 2, 3, 4, 5, 6, 7, 8, 9, 10, 11, 12, 13, 14, 15, 16, 17, 18, 19, 20]
```

Discussion

This puzzle reveals a super concise method to generate an array of numbers from 1 to n using the powerful combination of arrow functions, the spread operator, and the map() method.

To start, we have a function called f that uses arrow function syntax. It takes a parameter n. The Array(n) part creates an empty array with a length equal to n. Then, we use the spread operator (...) to spread the elements of this array into a new one. Essentially, we end up with an array containing undefined elements from 0 to n-1.

Next, we use the map() method on the array we just created. The map() method is fantastic for transforming elements in an array. In this case, we transform each element using an arrow function (_, i) => i + 1. The arrow function takes two parameters: _ and i. We use the underscore as a convention to show that it's not going to be used in the function. The i represents the index of the current element in the array.

Now, the arrow function does something simple: it returns i + 1. By doing this, we add 1 to each element's index in the array. Since array indices start from 0, adding 1 gives us the numbers from 1 to n.

Lastly, the transformed array is returned as the output of the function. So, when you call the f function with a number like 5, it generates an array [1, 2, 3, 4, 5] and gives it back to you.

This code is an elegant way to generate number sequences using functional programming concepts in JavaScript. It takes advantage of some JavaScript shorthand syntax to achieve brevity.

Further Reading

The Array() constructor
https://developer.mozilla.org/en-US/docs/Web/JavaScript/Reference/Global_Objects/Array/Array

The spread (...) syntax
https://developer.mozilla.org/en-US/docs/Web/JavaScript/Reference/Operators/Spread_syntax

The map() method
https://developer.mozilla.org/en-US/docs/Web/JavaScript/Reference/Global_Objects/Array/map

The Chain Master

```javascript
const titles = null;
let x = 0;

titles?.[++x].toUpperCase();

console.log(x);
```

Guess the Output

Try to guess what the output is before moving to the next page.

This code will output:

```
0
```

Discussion

In this puzzle, we attempt to increment x by 1 through optional chaining, but since titles is null, the increment operation is not executed. So, it prints the value of x (which is still 0) to the console.

Let's dig a bit deeper. The ?. is called the optional chaining operator. It allows us to access properties or call methods on an object only if the object is not null or undefined. Since titles is null, the code after ?. will not be executed.

Inside the square brackets, we have ++x. This is a pre-increment operator, which means it increments the value of x by 1 before the expression is evaluated. However, this line is essentially skipped due to titles being null. So x remains 0 and is not changed.

The optional chaining operator (?.) was added to ECMAScript 2020 to help developers prevent errors that could occur when trying to access properties or call methods on non-existent or nullish values. Before the optional chaining operator was introduced, developers had to write longer and more complex code to perform this check, which often involved using conditional statements or ternary operators.

For example:

```
the_chain_master/the_chain_master_ex1.js
// Check if response has a data object
// and data has a user property
const response = {
  //…
};

// using the conditional statement
if (response && response.data) {
  const user = response.data.user;
}

// using the ternary operator
const user =
  (response ?
    (response.data ?
      response.data.user :
      undefined) :
    undefined);
```

The optional chaining operator simplifies this process by allowing developers to directly access properties or call methods on an object without worrying about potential null or undefined values:

```
the_chain_master/the_chain_master_ex2.js
const response = {};
const city = response?.data?.user?.city;

console.log(city);    // → undefined
```

This code tries to grab a property that's nested inside response, but it doesn't actually exist. Now, instead of freaking out and throwing an error, JavaScript just gives you an undefined value. The syntax is not only shorter but also easier to read.

Technically speaking, when you use response?.data, it's basically the same as response == null ? undefined : response.data. That little ?. thing is just a handy way to make it faster. And here's something to keep in mind: you can't use the optional chaining on the left side of an assignment:

```
the_chain_master/the_chain_master_ex3.js
const response = {};

response?.data = "abc";
// → SyntaxError: Invalid left-hand side in assignment
```

So, the optional chaining operator streamlines the process of accessing nested properties and methods within objects. This operator short-circuits the evaluation if any intermediary property is null or undefined, preventing runtime errors and allowing for cleaner, more reliable code that gracefully handles missing or incomplete data structures.

Further Reading

Error-free property chaining with ES2020 optional chaining operator
https://blog.logrocket.com/error-free-property-chaining-with-es2020-optional-chaining-operator/

The optional chaining (?.) operator
https://developer.mozilla.org/en-US/docs/Web/JavaScript/Reference/Operators/Optional_chaining

The Shape Shifter

the_shape_shifter/the_shape_shifter.js

```
const a = "f"<{};
const b = "F"<{};

console.log(a);
console.log(b);
```

Guess the Output

 Try to guess what the output is before moving to the next page.

This code will output:

```
false
true
```

Discussion

In JavaScript, when you use the < operator to compare values, it performs a process called *type coercion* to convert the values into a common type before making the comparison.

In this code snippet, we have a string "F" on the left side and an empty object {} on the right side. JavaScript does its magic and tries to convert these values into a common type. In this case, since there's a string "F" involved, the common type chosen is a string.

When JavaScript tries to convert the empty object {} into a string, it uses the object's default toString() method, which returns a string representation of the object. In this case, the empty object {} is converted into the string "[object Object]". So now we have the comparison "F" < "[object Object]".

When you compare strings using the < operator, it performs a lexicographic comparison. That means JavaScript examines the character codes (Unicode values) of the corresponding characters from left to right. In Unicode, the character code for "[" (opening square bracket) is greater than the character code for "F" (uppercase letter F).

Therefore, "F" is considered to be less than "[object Object]", and the expression "F" < "[object Object]" evaluates to true. On the other hand, the character "f" has a higher Unicode value than the character "[", so "f" is considered to be more than "[object Object]", and the comparison evaluates to false.

You can also transform this technique into a reusable function:

```
the_shape_shifter/the_shape_shifter_ex1.js
const isUpperCase = x => x < {};

isUpperCase("F");    // → true
isUpperCase("f");    // → false
```

Now, I want to mention that this code snippet is controversial and may not output correct results for non-letter characters. For example:

```
the_shape_shifter/the_shape_shifter_ex2.js
const isUpperCase = x => x < {};

isUpperCase("5");    // → true
```

It's more of a demonstration to explore the fascinating quirks of JavaScript's type coercion system. To accurately verify that a string has only uppercase letters, you can use the following function:

```
the_shape_shifter/the_shape_shifter_ex3.js
function isUpperCase(str) {
  return str === str.toUpperCase() &&
         str !== str.toLowerCase();
}
console.log(isUpperCase("7"));    // → false
console.log(isUpperCase("@"));    // → false
console.log(isUpperCase("F"));    // → true
```

This function checks if a given string contains only uppercase letters by comparing it to its uppercase and lowercase versions. It returns false only if the input string contains a non-alphabetic character or a lowercase character.

So, remember, JavaScript's type coercion can be a powerful feature, but it can also lead to unexpected behavior if not used carefully. To play it safe, it's usually better to stick with explicit methods and functions for string operations.

This way, your code becomes easier to read, you'll know what to expect, and you'll dodge bugs caused by sneaky type conversions. If you choose to use type coercion, make sure you fully understand the potential risks.

Further Reading

The toString() method
> developer.mozilla.org/en-US/docs/Web/JavaScript/Reference/Global_Objects/Object/toString

The toUpperCase() method
> developer.mozilla.org/en-US/docs/Web/JavaScript/Reference/Global_Objects/String/toUpperCase

The toLowerCase() method
> developer.mozilla.org/en-US/docs/Web/JavaScript/Reference/Global_Objects/String/toLowerCase

Alphabet Aerobics

alphabet_aerobics/alphabet_aerobics.js
```
for(i=9,a='';++i<36;)a+=i.toString(36)

console.log(a);
```

Guess the Output

Try to guess what the output is before moving to the next page.

This code will output:

```
abcdefghijklmnopqrstuvwxyz
```

Discussion

This JavaScript code is a clever way to create a string containing the English alphabet. It generates a string with lowercase letters by converting each number from 9 to 35 into a character and adding it to a growing string.

Let's start with the for loop:

```
for(i=9,a='';++i<36;)
```

This line sets up a loop that starts at 9 and goes up to 35:

1. i=9 sets the starting point for the loop.

2. a='' initializes the variable a as an empty string. This variable will be used to store the generated characters.

3. ++i<36 tells the loop to iterate as long as i is less than 36.

Inside the loop, this line does the real work:

```
a+=i.toString(36)
```

The toString() method can be called on a number to convert it into a string. This method takes an optional argument that specifies the base in which the number should be represented. If you don't provide an argument, it defaults to base 10 (decimal). In this case, we pass 36 to specify that the number should be converted into its string representation in base 36. For example:

```
let i = 10;
console.log(i.toString(36));    // → a
i = 11;
console.log(i.toString(36));    // → b
```

So, the code builds a string by appending the base-36 representation of each number to the a variable. It keeps doing this in each iteration of the loop, gradually building up a string with all the characters. Once the loop is done, the code will have created a string that contains all the lowercase letters from a to z.

What Is Base 36?

 Base 36 is a numeral system that uses 36 distinct symbols to represent numbers: the digits 0-9 and the letters A-Z (or a-z, depending on convention). Base 36 allows you to represent large numbers with fewer characters compared to base 10 (decimal) or base 16 (hexadecimal). For example, it can be helpful in generating compact URLs or unique keys or encoding data for storage or transmission.

So, the takeaway from this puzzle is that you don't have to type in each and every character you want to create. Instead, you can make use of the built-in JavaScript methods to automatically generate them through programming.

Further Reading

Overview of the base36 encoding scheme
> en.wikipedia.org/wiki/Base36

The toString() method of Number
> developer.mozilla.org/en-US/docs/Web/JavaScript/Reference/Global_Objects/Number/toString

Do You Trust Your Eyes?

do_you_trust_your_eyes/do_you_trust_your_eyes.js

```js
// Two strings containing similar characters

const str1 = "Château";
const str2 = "Château";

console.log(str1 === str2);
```

Guess the Output

 Try to guess what the output is before moving to the next page.

This code will output:

```
false
```

Discussion

Some characters may seem identical to our eyes, but the JavaScript engine has its own special way of looking at things. The reason this code outputs false is because the two words "Château" and "Château" are not exactly the same when it comes to how they're written, even though they look pretty similar.

In the first word, "Château," the letter "â" is represented by a single character, U+00E2 (LATIN SMALL LETTER A WITH CIRCUMFLEX). This character is encoded as a single code point.

But in the second word, "Château," things get a bit trickier. The letter "â" is actually made up of two characters. First, you have the regular letter "a," and then there's this sneaky little combining character called a "circumflex accent" that adds the hat-like thing on top of the "a".

In other words, the letter consists of U+0061 (LATIN SMALL LETTER A) combined with U+0302 (COMBINING CIRCUMFLEX ACCENT).

Now, even though these two words might look the same when you see them written down, JavaScript is pretty strict when it comes to comparing strings. It looks at the actual characters being used, and since the first word has a different character sequence than the second word, JavaScript considers them as not being equal. So that's why the code outputs false.

But worry not! You can put the strings in a standardized format so that they can be compared accurately by doing something called *normalization*. In JavaScript, you can achieve this using the normalize() method available on string objects. Here's an example of how you can normalize the strings and perform the comparison:

```
do_you_trust_your_eyes/do_you_trust_your_eyes_ex1.js
// Normalizing strings before comparison

const string1 = "Château";
const string2 = "Château";

const normalizedString1 = string1.normalize("NFC");
const normalizedString2 = string2.normalize("NFC");

console.log(normalizedString1 === normalizedString2);    // → true
```

The normalize() method makes sure that when comparing strings, they're always consistent, even when there are differences in how characters are made. You can pick a particular normalization form, and in our case, we go with NFC.

There are three other options we can give to normalize(), including NFD, NFKC, and NFKD. The choice of form depends on what your program needs, but usually, NFC is a safer bet for regular text because it works better with characters converted from older encodings.

Further Reading

Text Processing with JavaScript
   pragprog.com/titles/fkjavascript/text-processing-with-javascript/

JavaScript has a Unicode problem by Mathias Bynens
   mathiasbynens.be/notes/javascript-unicode

The normalize() method
   developer.mozilla.org/en-US/docs/Web/JavaScript/Reference/Global_Objects/String/normalize

Truth or Fiction?

truth_or_fiction/truth_or_fiction.js

```javascript
const arr = [1, 8, NaN, 15, ""];

const newArr = arr.filter(function(item) {
  return !!item
});

console.log(newArr);
```

Guess the Output

 Try to guess what the output is before moving to the next page.

This code will output:

```
[1, 8, 15]
```

Discussion

The code !! in JavaScript can be used as a quick way of converting a value into either true or false in a sneaky way. First, the ! symbol is the logical NOT operator. It negates the value that follows it. For example, !true would result in false, and !false would result in true.

Now, if we apply the ! operator twice, it's like saying "not not." It might sound weird, but it's actually a clever trick. The first ! flips the value, and the second ! flips it back to what it originally was.

The number 1 is considered a "truthy" value. So when we apply the ! operator once, it turns into false because we're saying "not 1." But when we apply the ! operator again, it flips it back to true because we're saying "not not 1."

So, it's a shorthand way of saying, "I want the boolean version of the number 1, please!" When you want to convert any value, whether it's a number, a string, or something else, into a true or false value. You just stick !! in front of it, and you get the boolean version. For example, !!0 would evaluate to false, !!NaN would evaluate to false, and !!"hello" would evaluate to true.

What Are Truthy and Falsy Values?

Truthy values are those that are considered true when evaluated as a boolean, whereas falsy values are deemed false. Here are the values considered falsy in JavaScript:

- 0 - The number zero
- 0n - The BigInt zero
- "" - An empty string
- null - Represents the absence of any object value
- undefined - Represents an undefined value
- NaN - Stands for "Not a Number" and represents an invalid or unrepresentable value

All other values, including non-empty strings, non-zero numbers, arrays, objects, and functions, are considered truthy.

The purpose of the function in this puzzle is to filter out the falsy values (NaN and an empty string) from the original array arr, creating a new array newArr that only contains the truthy values (numbers).

Inside the callback function, we used the expression !!item as a way to convert a value to its corresponding boolean representation. It essentially performs two boolean conversions, converting any truthy value to true and any falsy value to false.

The filter function uses the return value of the callback function to decide whether to include an element in the newArr. If the return value is true, the element is included; if it's false, the element is excluded.

Now, we can further shrink this code by using the arrow function:

```
truth_or_fiction/truth_or_fiction_ex1.js
const arr = [1, 8, NaN, 15, ""];

const newArr = arr.filter(i => i);

console.log(newArr);
// → [1, 8, 15]
```

In this version of the code, we're using the arrow function to just return the value from the array itself. Since NaN and the empty string are falsy, they undergo automatic conversion to false, leading to their elimination from the array.

So remember, you can use double exclamation marks (!!) as a shortcut for the Boolean() function. And when you're working on filtering out falsy values, the arrow function can be handy in making your code shorter.

Further Reading

The logical NOT (!) operator
> https://developer.mozilla.org/en-US/docs/Web/JavaScript/Reference/Operators/Logical_NOT

Arrow function expressions
> https://developer.mozilla.org/en-US/docs/Web/JavaScript/Reference/Functions/Arrow_functions

On or Off?

on_or_off/on_or_off.js

```
let response = "on",
state = {on: 1, off: 0}[response]

console.log(state);
```

Guess the Output

Try to guess what the output is before moving to the next page.

This code will output:

```
1
```

Discussion

Suppose you have a light switch that can be turned on or off. You receive a response from a user indicating the current state of the switch:

```
let userResponse = "on";
```

When you're faced with the need to make decisions or run different blocks of code depending on specific conditions, the trusty if...else statement comes in handy:

```
let response = "on";
let state;

if (response === "on"){
  state = 1;
} else if (response === "off"){
  state = 0;
}
```

But the syntax can sometimes get a bit wordy. Some developers make the code shorter by using the ternary operator:

```
let response = "on";
let state = (response === "on") ? 1 : (response === "off") ? 0 : undefined;
```

In this teaser, we're using an extra nifty trick to make the code even more compact! We use an object to map the response to corresponding state values: "on" maps to 1 and "off" maps to 0.

Here's what's happening: in JavaScript, when using square brackets to access an object property, the value inside the brackets is treated as a key. So, {on:1, off:0}[response] is essentially accessing the value of the property whose key matches the value of the response. Since the response is "on", the expression evaluates to {on:1, off:0}["on"], which returns the value 1. It's like a hack to squeeze out some extra brevity.

Further Reading

The Object type
  https://developer.mozilla.org/en-US/docs/Web/JavaScript/Reference/Global_Objects/Object

The Grocery List

```javascript
const groceryList = [];

groceryList[0] = "Bread";
groceryList[1] = "Milk";
groceryList.user = "John";

console.log(groceryList.length);
```

Guess the Output

 Try to guess what the output is before moving to the next page.

You might have expected that the output would be 3, but this code will actually output 2.

Discussion

In this puzzle, the array initially starts as an empty array, like an empty bucket. Then, we start filling up the array. We put the string "Bread" in the first position of the array using groceryList[0] = "Bread". So now, the bucket has one thing in it: the "Bread".

Next, we put the string "Milk" in the second position of the array with groceryList[1] = "Milk". Now, the bucket has two things: the "Bread" and "Milk". But here's the tricky part: we also try to be sneaky and add a property to the array called "user", and we give it the value "John". It's like sticking a little note on the bucket.

When we ask the array how many things it has inside using groceryList.length, it ignores the sneaky little note. It counts only the actual elements inside the array, not the extra properties. Since we have two actual elements, the strings "Bread" and "Milk", the length of the array is 2.

You can also add properties to an array using the bracket notation, just like you would with a regular object:

```
const groceryList = [];

groceryList[0] = "Bread";
groceryList[1] = "Milk";
groceryList["user"] = "John";

console.log(groceryList.length);    // → 2
```

Here, because "user" is a string, it gets included as a property within the array.

So, properties are like extra information we can attach to an array or any other object, but they are not considered part of the array's length or elements. They are simply properties of the underlying object that happens to be an array. You also won't be able to iterate over these properties using array iteration methods like forEach() or map().

Further Reading

The Array object
https://developer.mozilla.org/en-US/docs/Web/JavaScript/Reference/Global_Objects/Array

Negative Gravity

negative_gravity/negative_gravity.js
```
console.log(7 - - 5)
console.log(7 - -5)
console.log(7- -5)
console.log(7--5)
```

Guess the Output

 Try to guess what the output is before moving to the next page.

This code will output:

```
12
12
12
SyntaxError: invalid increment/decrement operand
```

Discussion

The minus sign (-) is usually used for subtraction, but here we have two minus signs next to each other. So, the - is applied twice to the second operand, effectively negating the value twice. Since negating a negative number results in a positive number, the expression 7 - - 5 is effectively interpreted as 7 - (-5), which simplifies to 7 + 5. Consequently, the expression evaluates to the number 12.

The expression on the second line, 7 - -5, is similar to the first one. It correctly subtracts the value -5 from 7. The result is 12. 7- -5 also correctly subtracts the value -5 from 7. Just like the previous two expressions, the result is 12.

The fourth expression, 7--5, is different. There are two consecutive minus signs without any space in between. In JavaScript, -- is treated as the decrement operator, which is used to decrease a variable's value by 1. Since there are no variables here, this expression will result in a syntax error because it's not a valid operation.

So, similar to mathematical operations in the real world, subtracting a negative number from another number is equivalent to adding the positive value of that number. But, there is a caveat when there's no space between the first minus sign and the second one, in which case the expression is interpreted as the decrement operator.

Further Reading

The decrement operator
https://developer.mozilla.org/en-US/docs/Web/JavaScript/Reference/Operators/Decrement

The subtraction operator
https://developer.mozilla.org/en-US/docs/Web/JavaScript/Reference/Operators/Subtraction

Part II

Crafting Puzzles

Crafting Your Own JavaScript Puzzle

JavaScript is a fascinating language known for its quirks and unique behaviors. Writing puzzles is a fantastic way to better understand these quirks, unleash your creativity, and have fun!

I invite you to join in on the adventure and craft your very own puzzles to share with the JavaScript community. You can post them on programming forums, social media, or even the DevTalk page of the book![5] If you're wondering how to create the best JavaScript brain teasers, here are some tips to get you started:

- *Set a Clear Goal:* Start by defining what you want your puzzle to achieve. Is it about conquering asynchronous concepts, understanding scope, mastering functions, or diving into more advanced concepts? Make sure your puzzle lines up with the specific topic you want your fellow learners to grasp.

- *Create an Engaging Scenario:* Create a scenario or problem context for the puzzle. This could be a real-world problem or a fictional situation. The story or situation you come up with should be intriguing and directly related to your learning goal.

- *Formulate the Challenge:* Your puzzle should be a clever test of the targeted programming concept. Strive for that sweet spot—a challenge that's thought-provoking without causing hair-pulling frustration.

- *Try It Out Yourself:* Be sure to solve your own puzzle using your proposed solution. Test it with different inputs and edge cases to identify any issues.

- *Pack in the Learning:* Add explanations of the core concepts, sprinkle in code snippets with helpful comments, and provide links to resources that eager learners can dig into.

- *Share and Gather Feedback:* Once your puzzle is polished and gleaming, share it with us! Embrace the feedback from fellow coders to fine-tune your creation and make it even better.

---

5. https://devtalk.com/books/javascript-brain-teasers

Designing a JavaScript brain teaser can be a great way to engage with the coding community and encourage learning. It's all about igniting curiosity. Remember, your puzzles should be both challenging and rewarding, paving the way for others to upskill and enjoy the journey.

May I Request a Favor from You?

Thank you for taking the time to read this book! May I request a favor? Could you spare a minute to write a brief comment about this book on Amazon or Goodreads? Your feedback is incredibly valuable, not just to me as an author but to potential readers as well. I make it a point to read all reviews and greatly appreciate sincere feedback. To me, the true reward for my efforts is the knowledge that I'm making a positive impact on the JavaScript community.

Thanks again, and I really look forward to reading your feedback!

Index

Thank you!

We hope you enjoyed this book and that you're already thinking about what you want to learn next. To help make that decision easier, we're offering you this gift.

Head on over to https://pragprog.com right now, and use the coupon code BUYANOTHER2024 to save 30% on your next ebook. Offer is void where prohibited or restricted. This offer does not apply to any edition of *The Pragmatic Programmer* ebook.

And if you'd like to share your own expertise with the world, why not propose a writing idea to us? After all, many of our best authors started off as our readers, just like you. With up to a 50% royalty, world-class editorial services, and a name you trust, there's nothing to lose. Visit https://pragprog.com/become-an-author/ today to learn more and to get started.

Thank you for your continued support. We hope to hear from you again soon!

The Pragmatic Bookshelf

SAVE 30%!
Use coupon code
BUYANOTHER2024

Text Processing with JavaScript

You might think of regular expressions as the holy
grail of text processing, but are you sure you aren't
just shoehorning them in where standard built-in solutions already exist and would work better? JavaScript
itself provides programmers with excellent methods
for text manipulation, and knowing how and when to
use them will help you write more efficient and perfor-
mant code. From extracting data from APIs to calculat-
ing word counts and everything in between, discover
how to pick the right tool for the job and make the
absolute most of it every single time.

Faraz K. Kelhini
(240 pages) ISBN: 9798888650332. $51.95
https://pragprog.com/book/fkjavascript

Modern Asynchronous JavaScript

JavaScript today must interact with data-intensive
APIs and networks. The solution is a program that can
work *asynchronously* instead of finishing tasks in order. In modern JavaScript, instead of callbacks you'll
use promises to improve your application's performance
and responsiveness. JavaScript features introduced
in ES2020, ES2021, and ESNext like Promise.allSet-
tled(), Promise.any(), and top-level await help you de-
velop small, fast, low-profile applications. With the
AbortController API, cancel a pending async request
before it has completed. *Modern Asynchronous Java-
Script* gives you an arsenal of tools to build programs
that always respond to user requests, recover quickly
from difficult conditions, and deliver maximum performance.

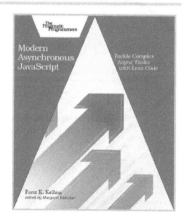

Faraz K. Kelhini
(77 pages) ISBN: 9781680509045. $14.99
https://pragprog.com/book/fkajs

Rust Brain Teasers

The Rust programming language is consistent and does its best to avoid surprising the programmer. Like all languages, though, Rust still has its quirks. But these quirks present a teaching opportunity. In this book, you'll work through a series of brain teasers that will challenge your understanding of Rust. By understanding the gaps in your knowledge, you can become better at what you do and avoid mistakes. Many of the teasers in this book come from the author's own experience creating software. Others derive from commonly asked questions in the Rust community. Regardless of their origin, these brain teasers are fun, and let's face it: who doesn't love a good puzzle, right?

Herbert Wolverson
(138 pages) ISBN: 9781680509175. $18.95
https://pragprog.com/book/hwrustbrain

Pandas Brain Teasers

This book contains 25 short programs that will challenge your understanding of Pandas. Like any big project, the Pandas developers had to make some design decisions that at times seem surprising. This book uses those quirks as a teaching opportunity. By understanding the gaps in your knowledge, you'll become better at what you do. Some of the teasers are from the author's experience shipping bugs to production, and some from others doing the same. Teasers and puzzles are fun, and learning how to solve them can teach you to avoid programming mistakes and maybe even impress your colleagues and future employers.

Miki Tebeka
(110 pages) ISBN: 9781680509014. $18.95
https://pragprog.com/book/d-pandas

Numerical Brain Teasers

Challenge your brain with math! Using nothing more than basic arithmetic and logic, you'll be thrilled as answers slot into place. Whether purely for fun or to test your knowledge, you'll sharpen your problem-solving skills and flex your mental muscles. All you need is logical thought, a little patience, and a clear mind. There are no gotchas here. These puzzles are the perfect introduction to or refresher for math concepts you may have only just learned or long since forgotten. Get ready to have more fun with numbers than you've ever had before.

Erica Sadun

(186 pages) ISBN: 9781680509748. $18.95

https://pragprog.com/book/esbrain

Go Brain Teasers

This book contains 25 short programs that will challenge your understanding of Go. Like any big project, the Go developers had to make some design decisions that at times seem surprising. This book uses those quirks as a teaching opportunity. By understanding the gaps in your knowledge, you'll become better at what you do. Some of the teasers are from the author's experience shipping bugs to production, and some from others doing the same. Teasers and puzzles are fun, and learning how to solve them can teach you to avoid programming mistakes and maybe even impress your colleagues and future employers.

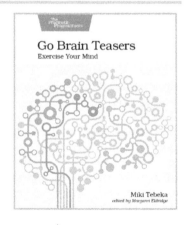

Miki Tebeka

(110 pages) ISBN: 9781680508994. $18.95

https://pragprog.com/book/d-gobrain

Hands-on Rust

Rust is an exciting new programming language combining the power of C with memory safety, fearless concurrency, and productivity boosters—and what better way to learn than by making games. Each chapter in this book presents hands-on, practical projects ranging from "Hello, World" to building a full dungeon crawler game. With this book, you'll learn game development skills applicable to other engines, including Unity and Unreal.

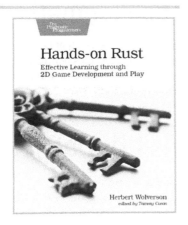

Herbert Wolverson
(342 pages) ISBN: 9781680508161. $47.95
https://pragprog.com/book/hwrust

Programming WebAssembly with Rust

WebAssembly fulfills the long-awaited promise of web technologies: fast code, type-safe at compile time, execution in the browser, on embedded devices, or anywhere else. Rust delivers the power of C in a language that strictly enforces type safety. Combine both languages and you can write for the web like never before! Learn how to integrate with JavaScript, run code on platforms other than the browser, and take a step into IoT. Discover the easy way to build cross-platform applications without sacrificing power, and change the way you write code for the web.

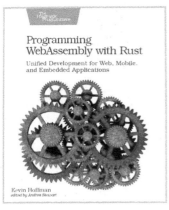

Kevin Hoffman
(238 pages) ISBN: 9781680506365. $45.95
https://pragprog.com/book/khrust

The Pragmatic Bookshelf

The Pragmatic Bookshelf features books written by professional developers for professional developers. The titles continue the well-known Pragmatic Programmer style and continue to garner awards and rave reviews. As development gets more and more difficult, the Pragmatic Programmers will be there with more titles and products to help you stay on top of your game.

Visit Us Online

This Book's Home Page
https://pragprog.com/book/fkjsbrain
Source code from this book, errata, and other resources. Come give us feedback, too!

Keep Up-to-Date
https://pragprog.com
Join our announcement mailing list (low volume) or follow us on Twitter @pragprog for new titles, sales, coupons, hot tips, and more.

New and Noteworthy
https://pragprog.com/news
Check out the latest Pragmatic developments, new titles, and other offerings.

Save on the ebook

Save on the ebook versions of this title. Owning the paper version of this book entitles you to purchase the electronic versions at a terrific discount.

PDFs are great for carrying around on your laptop—they are hyperlinked, have color, and are fully searchable. Most titles are also available for the iPhone and iPod touch, Amazon Kindle, and other popular e-book readers.

Send a copy of your receipt to support@pragprog.com and we'll provide you with a discount coupon.

Contact Us

Online Orders:	*https://pragprog.com/catalog*
Customer Service:	*support@pragprog.com*
International Rights:	*translations@pragprog.com*
Academic Use:	*academic@pragprog.com*
Write for Us:	*http://write-for-us.pragprog.com*